W9-ARJ-655

Pebble®

My Family

Single-Parent Families

by Sarah L. Schuette

Consulting Editor: Gail Saunders-Smith, PhD

MCL FOR
NEPTUNE CITY
PUBLIC LIBRARY

CAPSTONE PRESS
a capstone imprint

Pebble Books are published by Capstone Press,
151 Good Counsel Drive, P.O. Box 669, Mankato, Minnesota 56002.
www.capstonepress.com

Copyright © 2010 by Capstone Press, a Capstone imprint.
All rights reserved. No part of this publication may be reproduced in whole or in
part, or stored in a retrieval system, or transmitted in any form or by any means,
electronic, mechanical, photocopying, recording, or otherwise, without
written permission of the publisher.
For information regarding permission, write to Capstone Press,
151 Good Counsel Drive, P.O. Box 669, Dept. R, Mankato, Minnesota 56002.

Printed in the United States of America in North Mankato, Minnesota
092009
005618CGS10

Books published by Capstone Press are manufactured with paper
containing at least 10 percent post-consumer waste.

Library of Congress Cataloging-in-Publication Data
Schuette, Sarah L., 1976–
    Single-parent families / by Sarah L. Schuette.
    p. cm. — (Pebble books. My family)
    Includes bibliographical references and index.
    Summary: "Simple text and photographs present single-parent families,
including how family members interact with one another" — Provided by publisher.
    ISBN 978-1-4296-3980-4 (library binding)
    ISBN 978-1-4296-4838-7 (paperback)
    1. Single parents — Juvenile literature. 2. Family — Juvenile literature. I. Title.
II. Series.
HQ759.915.S38 2010
306.85'6 — dc22   2009023390

Note to Parents and Teachers

The My Family set supports national social studies standards
related to identifying family members and their roles in the
family. This book describes and illustrates single-parent families.
The images support early readers in understanding the text. The
repetition of words and phrases helps early readers learn new
words. This book also introduces early readers to subject-specific
vocabulary words, which are defined in the Glossary section. Early
readers may need assistance to read some words and to use the
Table of Contents, Glossary, Read More, Internet Sites, and Index
sections of the book.

Table of Contents

Single Parents

Parents raise children.
Single-parent families
have one parent.

mother

son

daughter

5

Some children live
with their mother.
Other children live
with their father.

Helping

Members of single-parent families help each other. Kim helps her mother make soup for dinner.

Amy's mother teaches her
to play the guitar.

Having Fun

Members of single-parent families have fun together. Peter and John play hide-and-seek with their dad.

Shelly and her mother
play golf.

Carlos and his dad play
at the pool.

Beth and her dad
have a picnic.
They eat watermelon.

Members of single-parent families love each other.

Glossary

father — a male parent

golf — a game in which players use special clubs to hit a small ball into holes on a course

member — a part of a group or family

mother — a female parent

parent — a mother or a father

raise — to look after children until they are grown up

single — one

Donahue, Jill L. *Dad's Shirt.* Read-it! Readers. Minneapolis: Picture Window Books, 2007.

Schaefer, Lola M. *Fathers.* Families. Mankato, Minn.: Capstone Press, 2008.

Sirett, Dawn. *Mommy Loves Me.* New York: DK, 2006.

Internet Sites

FactHound offers a safe, fun way to find Internet sites related to this book. All of the sites on FactHound have been researched by our staff.

Here's all you do:

Visit *www.facthound.com*

FactHound will fetch the best sites for you!

Index

Word Count: 89
Grade: 1
Early-Intervention Level: 10

Editorial Credits
Gillia Olson, editor; Juliette Peters, designer; Sarah Schuette, photo stylist;
    Marcy Morin, studio scheduler; Eric Manske, production specialist

Photo Credits
All photos by Capstone Studio/Karon Dubke

The Capstone Press Photo Studio thanks Countryside Homes, in Mankato, Minn.,
for its help with photo shoots for this book.

The author dedicates this book to her parents, Willmar and Jane Schuette.